Phyllo

Easy Recipes for Sweet and Savory Treats

Jill O'Connor

Photography by Susan Marie Anderson
and Christopher Conrad

CHRONICLE BOOKS

SAN FRANCISCO

Acknowledgments

Thank you to Leslie Jonath, who is a great editor and always so encouraging. To my parents for letting me turn their entire house into one big test kitchen; to the ladies at Hicklebee's for tasting, testing, and enjoying as much phyllo as I could stuff them with; and to Eileen Healey for giving me the tools I needed to finish this project.

Text copyright © 1997 by Jill O'Connor
Photographs copyright © 1997 by Susan Marie Anderson, front cover and pages 6-7, 18-19, 30, 33, 36, 42, 50, 56-57, 68, and 79
Photographs copyright © 1997 by Christopher Conrad, pages 23, 26, 39, 45, 53, 60, 65, 71, 76, 80, 85, and 89

Food styling by Patty Wittmann

Book design by Martine Trélaün

Printed in Hong Kong

Distributed in Canada by Raincoast Books
8680 Cambie Street
Vancouver, B.C. V6P 6M9

10 9 8 7 6 5 4 3 2

Chronicle Books
85 Second Street
San Francisco, CA 94105

Web Site: www.chronbooks.com

Library of Congress Cataloging-in-Publication Data:
O'Connor, Jill.
    Phyllo: easy recipes for sweet and savory treats/by Jill O'Connor; photography Susan Marie Anderson and Christopher Conrad.
        p. cm.
    Includes index.
    ISBN 0-8118-1019-4 (pb)
    1. Cookery (Filo dough). I. Title.

TX770.F55O26 1996
641.8—dc20
                                        96-11107
                                        CIP

For sweet Olivia

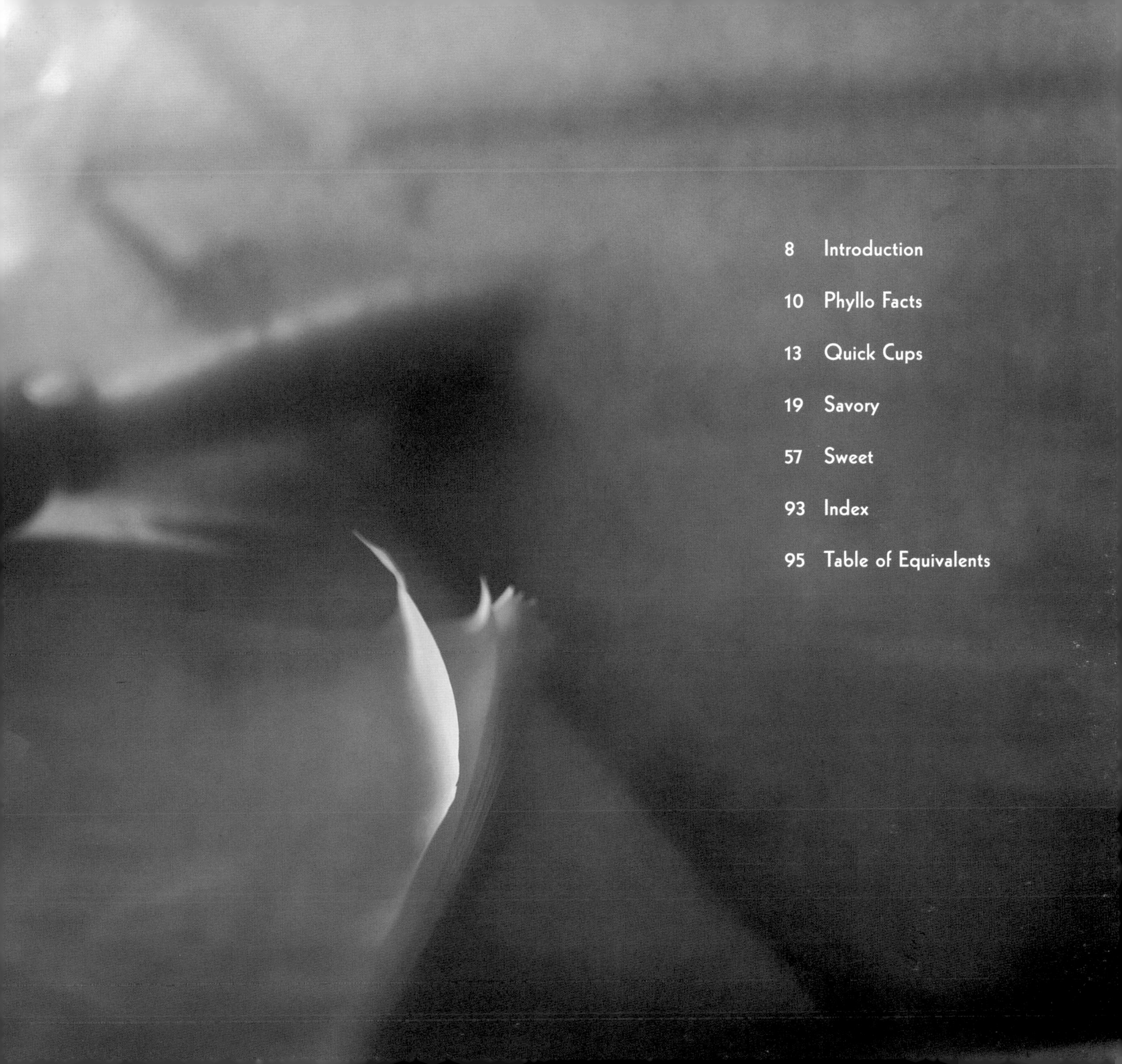

From pie crust to pâte à choux, pastry making intimidates experienced and novice cooks alike. It's tricky; it requires time, precision, and sometimes just the right touch. There is one pastry dough, however, that is easy to use, versatile, and accessible to every cook: phyllo.

Phyllo (from *phyllon*, which means "leaf" in Greek) is paper-thin sheets of dough made from flour, water, and a bit of oil. When these pastry sheets are brushed lightly with melted butter or oil and layered, they can enclose both sweet and savory fillings. The resulting pastries are incomparably light, crisp, and flavorful. Traditionally used in Greek and Middle Eastern cooking for dishes such as spanakopita and baklava, phyllo is very flexible and performs beautifully in a range of regional and international dishes, from quesadillas to fruit crumbles.

Although it is possible to make phyllo dough yourself, it is truly an art. In some Greek villages the preparation of phyllo dough is often a communal effort, similar to the preparation of strudel dough in Eastern Europe. It requires the efforts of many to gently pull and stretch the dough to just the right consistency. With skill and infinite patience, the phyllo dough is stretched thinner and thinner over the backs of many hands, until one piece of dough covers and drapes an entire table as if it were an edible tablecloth. The phyllo is considered perfect when it is nearly transparent and each worker can clearly see his or her fingers through the filmy dough.

For the recipes in this book, I used the phyllo dough that is readily available in most supermarkets. Fresh phyllo is often available in Greek, Middle Eastern, and some international markets in larger cities. It is well worth seeking out if you can find it, as it is often even easier to work with than dough that has been frozen and thawed. Phyllo sheets that have been pre-buttered are also available from some markets that specialize in fresh phyllo. This makes baking with phyllo even quicker, and especially stress-free for the beginner.

Phyllo is probably one of the most misunderstood members of the pastry world. Thought of as difficult and temperamental to work with, many cooks avoid it. But baking with phyllo is actually very simple, and like modeling clay it can be twisted, rolled, folded, bent, and pressed into a variety of fanciful and geometrically precise shapes.

Phyllo can easily stand in for its more difficult cousins, strudel dough and puff pastry. It can take center stage, as it does in the classic triangular Mediterranean Chicken Turnovers, or it can play the supporting role as it does in Venetian Napoleons, separating voluptuous layers of mascarpone cheese and sweetened strawberries that are laced with port and balsamic vinegar. Phyllo can create sweet and savory strudels, as well as innovative napoleons and mille-feuilles.

Layered squares of buttered phyllo pressed into miniature to mammoth muffin tins form cups, or "nests." These cups can hold sweet fillings such as fresh fruit or ice cream, or savory fillings such as black bean chili or crumbled blue cheese and caramelized onions. Phyllo can stand in for pâte brisée to line a pie dish, or be molded free-form into a simple yet beautiful tart shell.

Experienced chefs and pastry chefs continue to experiment with phyllo, creating new and innovative methods for using it. I have eaten small phyllo-wrapped "purses" of nutty wild rice accompanying roasted game hens, cracked the phyllo crust enclosing a buttery, herbed salmon fillet, and delighted in a luscious phyllo-wrapped potato strudel enriched with crème fraîche, garlic, and fresh thyme. One enterprising pastry chef even invented a chocolate phyllo pastry by sprinkling confectioners' sugar and cocoa powder between the buttered sheets of dough before baking.

Easy to find and inexpensive to buy, phyllo provides every cook, even those who have never baked, with an interesting and enjoyable pastry-making experience. Dishes made with phyllo are always exciting; they are perfect for the grandest social event or for the simplest, rustic supper. Phyllo never disappoints. It is impressive to present and always delivers a deliciously flaky, gorgeous result that belies its essential simplicity.

Preparation and Equipment

Before starting out, make sure you have a large flat surface to work on, and that it, and all your necessary equipment, is clean and dry. Have the following equipment and ingredients ready:

A sharp knife

A knife with a serrated edge

A good-quality pastry brush

A ruler to measure the phyllo before cutting

A light cotton dish cloth or
    heavy paper towels

Parchment paper or aluminum foil
    to line baking sheets

Baking sheets with and without sides

A large metal spatula

Melted butter, clarified butter,
    or oil, or vegetable-oil spray

Granulated or confectioners' sugar (if using)

Bread crumbs, cookie crumbs, or
    chopped nuts (if using)

Filling (for stuffed phyllo pastries)

Working with Phyllo

The essential skill necessary for working successfully with phyllo dough is speed. Because the sheets of dough are paper-thin and delicate, they dry out quickly when exposed to air and will crack and crumble. Organization and practice will help you to avoid this pitfall.

If you are using frozen phyllo dough, thaw it in the refrigerator for at least 24 hours. Allow the dough to sit at room temperature for another 2 or 3 hours before removing it from its packaging and preparing the pastry. This process may seem tedious, but if you follow these simple steps your phyllo will be smooth and supple and the delicate sheets will not stick together.

Because phyllo dries out so quickly, carefully open the package and remove only the number of sheets necessary for the recipe you are preparing (you can approximate if counting is tedious). Carefully reroll the remaining dough, wrap it tightly in plastic wrap, and store it in the refrigerator for up to 1 month.

You can prepare phyllo pastries anytime, but the hotter and drier the weather, the faster the phyllo will become dry, brittle, and unworkable. If possible, prepare phyllo pastries on a cool day, especially if you are a beginner. This will give you a little extra working time before the phyllo becomes too dry to handle.

Make sure your filling is completely prepared and cooled before starting any phyllo pastry that will be filled before baking. A filling that is even slightly warm will wilt the pastry and make breaking and tearing more likely to happen.

Wet a very light cotton dish cloth or a few heavy paper towels with cool water and ring out until just barely damp. After removing a sheet of phyllo, lay the cloth or towels over the remaining sheets of phyllo while you are working. Once you become more adept with phyllo and your preparation speed increases, you can dispense with this step.

When buttering or oiling the pastry sheets, begin by brushing the edges first to prevent them from cracking. Work quickly towards the center of the sheet. Do not drench each sheet with butter or oil, but make sure the dough is evenly and lightly covered before you lay on the next sheet of phyllo. Do not worry if the sheets buckle slightly or have a few folds in them as you layer; the most important thing is to make sure your sheets of phyllo are brushed and layered quickly. If a phyllo sheet rips while you are working with it, simply "glue" it together with some melted butter or oil. If it is the final sheet in your stack, lay an unripped sheet over the torn one before continuing with the recipe. Before baking, brush the finished phyllo pastry form, whether it is a triangle, purse, or strudel, with some melted butter or oil to protect it and to ensure even browning.

Savory phyllo pastries can usually be baked on an ungreased baking sheet without sticking. Lining a baking sheet with parchment paper or aluminum foil may be advised if a particularly sticky or gooey filling is used, to prevent any possible spillage from burning or sticking. Sweet phyllo pastries should always be baked on parchment-lined baking sheets. Since sweet pastries are often sprinkled liberally with sugar to yield a crisp, caramelized finish, they can easily burn or at least stick to an unlined baking sheet making it nearly impossible to remove the pastry without breaking it.

Ingredients

Depending on the recipe, melted salted or unsalted butter, clarified butter, olive oil, vegetable oils or vegetable oil sprays, and flavored oils can be used to brush onto the layers of phyllo dough. Clarified butter, which is simply melted butter with all the milk solids removed, creates an extra-crisp and flaky pastry. However, it takes more time to prepare clarified butter and you will need a larger amount of butter to begin with. If possible, use only unsalted butter for sweet pastries.

To make clarified butter, slowly melt the butter in a large, heavy saucepan over low heat. Remove the pan from the heat and scrape off the foam. Slowly pour the golden oil into a separate container and discard the pale solids left behind in the pan. One pound of butter will yield approximately 1 ½ cups of clarified butter. When using regular melted butter, you can do a little "mini-clarifying" by dipping your pastry brush only in the top portion of the melted butter, discarding the milk solids as you get to the bottom of the pan.

Savory pastries can be layered with a melted compound, or flavored butter such as garlic butter, sun-dried tomato butter, fresh herb butter, and even butter flavored with curry powder or anchovies (for the brave of heart). Mince the flavoring agents and stir them into melted butter.

Olive and vegetable oils flavored with ingredients from fresh or roasted garlic to basil, rosemary, and even porcini mushrooms are available in specialty foods stores. Purchase the flavored oils, or make them yourself to brush over layers of phyllo dough for a boost of flavor in savory pastries. Shredded Parmesan cheese can also be sprinkled in between the layers for extra flavor.

Sweet pastries benefit from having granulated or confectioners' sugar sprinkled over the butter in between the layers of phyllo. The baked phyllo will be sweet, crunchy, and extra crisp, enabling it to support creamy fillings and sauces without becoming soggy. Try sprinkling ground almonds, pecans, walnuts and even crumbled Italian amaretti cookies or crunchy gingersnap crumbs between the layers for additional flavor and texture.

Storing and Reheating

Before baking, phyllo pastries can be chilled for 1 day or frozen for up to 1 month. To freeze, lay the phyllo pastries in a single layer on a baking sheet and freeze until firm. When frozen, wrap the pastries well with plastic wrap or place in freezer bags. To bake frozen pastries, do not thaw first. Thawing creates a soggy pastry. Simply bake the pastry, straight from the freezer, in a preheated 375-degree oven. The frozen pastries may take a minute or two longer to bake than stated in the recipe. Phyllo hors d'oeuvres, which are time-consuming to prepare, are wonderful baked straight from the freezer. This allows any harried host or hostess to make up a huge quantity of various pastries ahead of time to have on hand for impromptu and stress-free entertaining.

Do not reheat baked phyllo pastries in the microwave. This will make them limp and soggy. Reheat previously baked phyllo pastry uncovered on a baking sheet in a 350-degree oven until the phyllo is crisp and the filling is warm.

Paper-thin and light-as-a-feather pastry cups can be molded from phyllo dough and baked ahead of time to hold a wide variety of savory and sweet fillings. They are a snap to make and lovely to serve. The three most common sizes of muffin tins, jumbo (top diameter of 3 ½ to 4 inches), standard (top diameter of 3 inches), and miniature (top diameter of 1 ½ to 2 inches), are perfect for making large quantities of these cups in one sitting. The miniature phyllo cups are perfect for bite-sized hors d'oeuvres, and the bigger cups can hold individual dessert portions or quick entrées.

To prepare the phyllo cups:

1. Preheat the oven to 325 degrees F. Layer 4 sheets of phyllo dough, brushing each layer with melted butter or oil. To prepare cups for a dessert filling, sprinkle each layer with granulated or confectioners' sugar after brushing it with butter or oil.

2. Cut squares from the phyllo (3 ½-inch squares for mini cups; 5 ½-inch squares for standard cups; 8-inch squares for jumbo cups). Spray the muffin tins with a vegetable-oil spray.

3. Press the layered phyllo squares gently but firmly against the bottoms and sides of the muffin cups.

4. Bake the empty shells until they are crisp and golden, about 7 to 10 minutes. Remove them from the oven and let them cool completely before filling. The cups can be prepared and baked 2 to 3 days in advance and stored in a covered airtight container.

Savory Quick Cup Fillings

Black bean and chicken chili with sour cream, salsa, and fresh cilantro

Diced lamb loin sautéed with chilies, garlic, and fresh mint

Sun-dried tomatoes, crumbled goat cheese, and capers

Crumbled Roquefort cheese, blanched asparagus tips, and herbes de Provence

Tandoori chicken bits with cucumber raita

Warm Camembert and mango chutney

Halved cherry tomatoes, diced cucumbers, and Kalamata olives with an oregano vinaigrette

Eggs scrambled with bits of smoked salmon, topped with sour cream and red and black caviar

Crumbled cooked Italian sausage with pesto and roasted peppers

Mushroom duxelles

Crab salad

Smoked oysters, crumbled Stilton cheese, and fresh chives

Grilled lemon-herb chicken with oven-roasted root vegetables

Crumbled bacon, diced fresh tomato, and guacamole

Bay shrimp in fresh dill mayonnaise or vinaigrette

Flaked smoked salmon, crème fraîche, diced red onion, and capers

Smoked trout with horseradish cream

Shredded barbecued pork and creamy coleslaw

Caponata (Italian eggplant relish)

Curried cashew-chicken salad

Melted Fontina cheese chunks and tomato chutney

Chicken cooked in Thai peanut sauce with slivered green onions and grated carrots

Sweet Quick Cup Fillings

Strawberries marinated in fresh orange juice and Grand Marnier, topped with whipped cream

Vanilla ice cream topped with fudge sauce and chopped salted almonds

Vanilla ice cream with toasted hazelnuts, topped with fresh raspberries and drizzled with Frangelico liqueur

Coconut ice cream topped with a compote of diced fresh kiwi, pineapple, and papaya that has been marinated in lime juice and dark rum and sprinkled with flaked coconut

Crème pâtissière with fresh cherries and kirsch

Pecan pie

Raspberry and passion fruit sorbet

Chocolate soufflé

Grand Marnier soufflé

Chocolate mousse topped with whipped cream and garnished with candied violets and chopped pistachios

Whole-milk or low-fat ricotta cheese and fresh peaches drizzled with honey

Apples sautéed with brown sugar and Calvados and topped with a dollop of crème fraîche

Ambrosia (mandarin orange segments, pineapple, miniature marshmallows, and pecans tossed with lightly sweetened sour cream or plain yogurt and freshly grated coconut)

Fresh blueberries, raspberries, and blackberries with sweetened mascarpone cheese

Vanilla ice cream or frozen yogurt topped with bananas sautéed in butter and brown sugar

Note

To prepare the pecan pie or the chocolate and Grand Marnier soufflés, fill the pastry cups with the pie or soufflé mixture before baking them.

Reducing Fat

If you are interested in reducing the sometimes substantial fat content of many phyllo pastries, try substituting butter-flavored or olive oil cooking spray for the melted butter or olive oil called for in most recipes. Simply spray the phyllo lightly with the cooking spray instead of brushing it with melted butter or oil. Using a cooking spray also has the advantage of allowing you to work faster, especially when preparing sweet or savory phyllo cups.

You can substitute reduced-fat mayonnaise, hard cheeses, ricotta cheese, cream cheese, and sour cream for all or part of their higher-fat counterparts to help lower the fat content of your phyllo pastries. Phyllo cups filled with fruit sorbets, flavored yogurts, or frozen yogurt, and topped with fat-free fudge sauce or fruit coulis make mouth-watering, guilt-free indulgences. Sauté fresh fruit such as apples, pineapple, or pears in fruit juice concentrates spiked with cinnamon, vanilla bean, or other spices instead of butter. Wrap the cooled cooked fruit in phyllo strudels or croustades for a tempting low-fat dessert.

For savory appetizers, fill miniature fat-free phyllo cups with delicious low-fat fillings:

Fat-free chili topped with plain yogurt, cilantro, and fresh salsa

Pureed white beans or chick-peas flavored with garlic, cumin, and lemon

Diced cherry tomatoes, cucumbers, fresh dill, and bay shrimp tossed with a feta cheese and yogurt dressing

Orzo tossed with shredded grilled marinated chicken breast, sautéed bell peppers, and onions

Diced grilled vegetables tossed with a balsamic vinaigrette

Lobster chunks, minced scallions and red peppers, and sweet corn, in a low-fat chipotle-chile mayonnaise

Notes

Four-Cheese Pie with Wild Mushrooms and Swiss Chard

Makes 8 to 10 servings

If wild mushrooms are unavailable, substitute an equal amount of button mushrooms. Try serving this vegetarian pie for a large group instead of lasagna or another casserole dish.

3 tablespoons butter, plus 8 tablespoons
   butter, melted
1 pound mixed wild and domestic mushrooms
   (shiitakes, portobellos, creminis, and oysters)
   cleaned and sliced
1 pound button mushrooms, cleaned and sliced
⅓ cup Madeira or red wine
¼ cup heavy cream
Salt and freshly ground pepper to taste

2 cups ricotta cheese
1 cup grated Parmesan cheese
1 cup grated Fontinella cheese (see note)
1 ½ cups grated Asiago cheese
1 clove garlic, crushed
¼ teaspoon ground or freshly grated nutmeg
2 large bunches red Swiss chard
14 sheets phyllo dough

Melt the 3 tablespoons butter in a large sauté pan or skillet over high heat. Add the mushrooms and cook, stirring occasionally, until they are tender and any liquid they have released is evaporated. Add the Madeira or red wine, stir to scrape the browned bits from the bottom of the pan, and cook until no liquid remains. Add the heavy cream and cook until the mixture is very thick. Season with salt and pepper. Remove from the heat and let cool completely.

In a medium bowl, combine the ricotta, Parmesan, Fontinella, and ½ cup of the Asiago. Stir in the garlic and nutmeg and season with pepper. Cover and refrigerate.

Wash the Swiss chard, removing any woody stems. Shake excess water from the leaves but do not dry completely. Heat a very large nonstick sauté pan or skillet over medium-high heat and add the damp chard. Season with salt and pepper. Cook, uncovered and stirring occasionally, until the chard is limp and tender. Drain any excess liquid, coarsely chop, and let cool completely.

Preheat the oven to 375 degrees F. To assemble the pie, brush a 13-by-9-by-2-inch pan with some of the melted butter. Place 1 sheet of phyllo dough in the pan, allowing the sheet to extend up the sides of the pan. Brush lightly with butter. Layer 5 more sheets of phyllo over the first, buttering each one. Refrigerate until the butter coating hardens, about 10 minutes.

Spoon the ricotta cheese mixture over the phyllo, spreading it evenly over the bottom. Top with the mushroom mixture and spread it evenly over the cheese. Finally, spread the cooked chard over the mushrooms and sprinkle with the remaining 1 cup Asiago cheese.

Using a sharp knife, trim the remaining 8 sheets of phyllo into 9-by-13-inch rectangles. Place 1 sheet of phyllo over the filling and brush with butter. Repeat with the remaining 7 sheets of phyllo, buttering each one.

Before baking, use a sharp knife to cut through the top layers of phyllo only to create a diamond pattern.

Bake until the phyllo is crisp and golden, 30 to 35 minutes. Let cool for 2 or 3 minutes before slicing and serving.

Note

Fontinella cheese is similar to fontina, only harder. It is usually available where Stella brand cheeses are sold. Fontina may be substituted for fontinella.

Spanakopita

Makes 8 to 10 servings

No phyllo book would be complete without a recipe for spanakopita. Mine requires the delicate flavor and texture of fresh spinach, sautéed and subtly seasoned with nutmeg. It is then combined with tangy feta cheese and rolled into an easy-to-prepare strudel.

1 tablespoon butter, plus ½ cup (1 stick) butter, melted

1 small onion, diced

2 cloves garlic, crushed

2 pounds fresh spinach, stemmed

⅛ teaspoon ground or freshly grated nutmeg

Salt and pepper to taste

1 cup (6 ounces) crumbled feta cheese

1 egg plus 1 egg yolk

3 tablespoons heavy cream

8 sheets phyllo dough

Preheat oven to 375 degrees F. In a large sauté pan or skillet, melt the 1 tablespoon butter over medium-high heat and cook the onion and garlic until they are fragrant and lightly browned, about 2 to 3 minutes. Add the spinach leaves and cook uncovered until they are limp and tender, and no liquid remains in the pan. Add the nutmeg and season with salt and pepper. Let cool completely.

In a large bowl, combine the feta, egg and egg yolk, and cream. Coarsely chop the spinach and stir it into the egg mixture.

Lay 1 sheet of phyllo dough flat on a work surface. Brush the phyllo lightly with the melted butter, working from the edges towards the center. Layer the remaining 7 sheets of phyllo over the first, lightly buttering each one.

Spoon the spinach mixture down the long edge of the phyllo, about 2 inches from the bottom and 1 inch in from each side. Fold the 2-inch flap of phyllo carefully over the filling and fold the sides over this. Roll the strudel up as you would a jelly roll, as tightly as possible. Brush it with butter and place it seam-side down on an ungreased baking sheet.

Bake until golden, 20 to 25 minutes. Let the strudel rest for 5 minutes. Using a serrated knife, slice it into 8 to 10 pieces. Serve warm.

Mediterranean Chicken Turnovers

Makes 28 turnovers

To give these delectable appetizers an extra boost of flavor, I like to season the chicken breasts with salt and pepper and lots of dried thyme before sautéing or grilling them. Poached or roasted chicken would also work well here.

2 cups diced cooked chicken breasts

¼ cup toasted pine nuts (see note)

½ cup roasted peppers (jarred peppers are fine), coarsely chopped

1 cup crumbled feta cheese

½ cup chopped fresh Italian parsley

1 tablespoon minced fresh thyme, or
   1 teaspoon dried thyme

3 cloves garlic, minced

Salt and pepper to taste

½ cup olive oil

2 cloves garlic, crushed (optional)

14 sheets phyllo dough

In a large bowl, combine the chicken, pine nuts, peppers, feta cheese, parsley, thyme, and garlic. Season with salt and pepper and stir well. Cover and refrigerate until ready to assemble the turnovers.

Preheat the oven to 375 degrees F. In a small bowl, combine the olive oil with the garlic, if you like. Lay flat 1 sheet of phyllo dough on a clean work surface. Lightly brush the phyllo with the olive oil, working from the edges towards the center. Lay a second sheet of phyllo over the first and brush with oil. Using a sharp knife, slice the phyllo into four 3-by-17 ½-inch strips.

Place about 2 tablespoons of the chicken filling 1 inch from the bottom of each strip. Starting with the first phyllo strip, fold 1 corner of the strip over the filling diagonally across to the opposite edge to form a triangle.

Continue folding the triangle up and over itself, as if you were folding up a flag, brushing the dry pastry with oil as you fold it up. Brush the completed triangle with oil and place it seam-side down on an ungreased baking sheet. Repeat with the remaining 3 strips of phyllo and then with the remaining 12 sheets. You should end up with a total of 28 turnovers.

Bake the turnovers for 15 to 17 minutes, or until golden brown. Serve them warm.

Note

To toast the pine nuts, cook them in a nonstick sauté pan or skillet over medium heat, stirring constantly, for 1 to 2 minutes until they begin to release their oils, become fragrant and start to brown. Let cool.

Pork and Pepper Jack Quesadillas

Makes 6 to 8 entrée servings or 16 appetizer servings

While living in San Diego I was seduced by the carnitas served at Porkyland, a modest Mexican food eatery where carnitas are a specialty. Succulent is the best word to describe these enticing bits of shredded pork. Here is my version, wrapped in phyllo. Serve small wedges of these quesadillas as an appetizer topped with sour cream, diced avocado, and salsa, or serve larger portions as an entrée with a salad of avocado and mixed baby lettuces spiked with a spicy vinaigrette.

For the carnitas
5 pounds boneless pork butt (see note)
Salt and freshly ground pepper to taste
3 tablespoons vegetable oil
2 medium onions, diced
2 tablespoons dried oregano
1 teaspoon dried thyme
1 bay leaf

1 tablespoon ground cumin
5 cloves garlic, minced
4 cups water

24 sheets phyllo dough
½ to ¾ cup olive oil or melted butter
2 cups shredded pepper jack cheese
½ cup diced onion
1 cup fresh cilantro leaves

To prepare the carnitas, cut the pork into 10 large chunks, about 8 ounces each, and season generously with salt and pepper. Heat the oil in a large 6-quart stockpot or Dutch oven. Turning occasionally, brown the pork chunks over medium to medium-high heat until the fat is rendered and the meat is a dark mahogany brown, about 30 minutes.

Transfer the pork to a clean plate. Discard all but 2 tablespoons of the fat in the pan and cook the onions in the drippings over medium heat until translucent. Add the oregano, thyme, bay leaf, cumin, and garlic to the

pan and continue to cook until the onions are limp and golden and the herbs and spices are fragrant. Add water and stir to scrape up the browned bits from the bottom of the pan. Bring the liquid to a boil and return the pork chunks to the pot. Reduce the heat to a simmer and cook the meat for 3 to 4 hours, or until it is very tender and can easily be shredded with a fork.

Remove the meat from the cooking liquid, reserving the liquid. Shred the meat into smaller chunks using 2 forks. Cover and chill the meat until ready to use.

Strain the cooking liquid through a sieve into a bowl. Chill the liquid until all the fat rises to the top and solidifies. Remove the fat and discard. Combine the chilled meat and the defatted cooking liquid (which is now firm and gelatinous, but will melt and moisten the meat and add flavor when baked in the quesadilla) and set aside.

Preheat the oven to 400 degrees F. Line 2 baking sheets with parchment paper or aluminum foil.

Lay 1 sheet of phyllo dough flat on a clean work surface. Brush the phyllo lightly with the oil or butter, working from the edges towards the center. Layer 2 more sheets of phyllo over the first, brushing each one lightly with oil or butter. Place one fourth of the cold shredded carnitas in the center of the phyllo. Top the meat with one fourth of the shredded cheese, onion, and cilantro leaves. Place 3 additional sheets of phyllo over the filling, brushing each one lightly with oil. Fold the edges of the phyllo together rolling them up toward the filling, enclosing the meat and forming a rough circle. Repeat this process with the remaining phyllo and filling ingredients to make 4 large quesadillas. Place 2 quesadillas on each baking sheet and bake them, 1 pan at a time, for 15 to 20 minutes, or until the phyllo is crisp and golden.

Cut the quesadillas into wedges and serve immediately.

Note

The 5 pounds of pork butt yields 2 pounds of shredded meat when cooked.

Grilled Vegetable Ratatouille Croustade

Makes 6 servings

Grilling the vegetables increases their sweetness and intensifies the flavor of this vegetarian entrée. If you substitute olive oil for the butter, this recipe will make an elegant dish for vegans as well.

1 large red onion, cut into ½-inch-thick slices

8 ounces (about 4) zucchini, cut lengthwise into ½-inch-thick slices

8 ounces (about 4) yellow squash, cut lengthwise into ½-inch-thick slices

12 ounces (about 4) Japanese eggplants, halved lengthwise

8 ounces (about 4) plum tomatoes

¼ cup olive oil or more as needed

Salt and pepper to taste

3 to 4 cloves garlic, chopped

½ cup roasted red peppers (jarred peppers are fine)

1 to 2 tablespoons balsamic vinegar

3 tablespoons fresh thyme leaves, minced

1 cup fresh basil leaves, shredded

9 sheets phyllo dough

Garlic Butter or Oil

½ cup (1 stick) butter, melted, or ½ cup olive oil

3 cloves garlic, crushed

Prepare hot coals for grilling. Secure the slices of onion with a bamboo skewer so that the rings stay together when grilled. Brush the onion, zucchini, squash, eggplants, and tomatoes liberally with olive oil and generously season with salt and pepper.

Grill the fresh vegetables until tender and lightly charred from the grill, about 5 to 7 minutes per side. (Cook the tomatoes only until the skins blister and blacken, about 10 minutes total.) Peel and coarsely chop the tomatoes and combine them with the garlic in a large bowl. Coarsely chop the remaining grilled vegetables and add them to the tomatoes with the roasted peppers, balsamic vinegar, and fresh herbs. Allow the filling to cool completely before assembling the croustade.

Preheat the oven to 375 degrees F. Lightly butter a 9-inch metal pie pan.

Lay 1 sheet of phyllo dough in the pie pan, letting the ends extend over the sides of the pan. To prepare the garlic butter or oil: combine the butter or oil and garlic in a small bowl. Brush the phyllo with garlic butter or oil. Layer 2 more sheets of phyllo over the first, brushing each one with the garlic butter or oil. Lay a fourth sheet of phyllo across the first 3 sheets, completely covering the bottom and sides of the pie pan. Brush the phyllo with the garlic butter or oil. Layer 2 more sheets of phyllo over this one, brushing each one with the garlic butter or oil.

Transfer the cooled ratatouille mixture to the pie pan and spread it evenly over the phyllo. Fold the flaps of phyllo over the filling. Brush 3 additional sheets of phyllo with the garlic butter or oil and loosely crumple each over the top of the pie, completely covering the filling. Loosely fold and crimp the flaps of phyllo extending over the rim around the crumpled phyllo topping. Drizzle the top of the croustade with any remaining garlic butter or oil.

Bake the croustade for 30 to 40 minutes, or until the phyllo is golden brown. Allow the pie to cool slightly before slicing it with a serrated knife.

Feta Cheese and Fresh Chive Phyllo Kisses

Makes 48 kisses

These delectable, flavor-packed cheese morsels freeze beautifully for do-ahead entertaining.

6 ounces feta cheese, crumbled

4 ounces cream cheese at room temperature

¼ cup grated Parmesan cheese

3 tablespoons snipped fresh chives

⅛ teaspoon ground or freshly grated nutmeg

Freshly ground pepper to taste

24 sheets phyllo dough

1 cup (2 sticks) butter, melted

In a medium bowl, stir the feta, cream cheese, Parmesan, chives, and nutmeg together until smooth. Season with ground pepper and refrigerate the mixture until firm enough to handle. Scoop the mixture by heaping teaspoons and roll into balls. Refrigerate the cheese balls until ready to use.

Cut 1 sheet of phyllo in half, crosswise, into two 8 ¾-by-12-inch pieces. Butter half of one of the pieces and place a cheese ball in the middle of the buttered half. Fold the unbuttered half over the cheese and carefully press the phyllo around the filling (as you would for ravioli). Butter the top and pull the 4 corners of the phyllo up around the cheese filling to form a small "kiss"-shaped pouch. Repeat this process with each of the remaining phyllo sheets.

Place the phyllo kisses on a baking sheet and press them gently onto the pan to flatten the bottoms of the pouches. (This will help the kisses hold their shape as they bake.) Because this particular pastry bakes and retains its shape better if it is frozen, freeze the pastries before you bake them. They should be frozen for at least 1 hour, and may be frozen for up to a month before baking.

Preheat the oven to 375 degrees F. Bake the frozen pastries for 10 to 12 minutes, or until they are golden brown and crisp. If the tops of the pastries brown too quickly, cover them loosely with a piece of aluminum foil and continue baking until done. Serve the kisses warm.

Pear, Gorgonzola, and Toasted Walnut Strudel

Makes 12 to 15 appetizer servings

The classic blend of ripe pears, pungent gorgonzola, and crisp walnuts flavors this sophisticated and versatile strudel. It is perfect served in small slices as an hors d'oeuvre with champagne, or as a first course presented with an endive salad. Or enjoy it as a British-style "savory" at the end of a meal, accompanied with small glasses of a robust, ruby-red port.

2 ripe but firm Bosc pears, peeled, halved, and cored

2 tablespoons Poire Williams or other pear brandy

2 tablespoons dark brown sugar

7 sheets phyllo dough

4 tablespoons (½ stick) butter, melted

3 tablespoons walnut oil

4 ounces Gorgonzola cheese, sliced or crumbled

½ cup coarsely chopped toasted walnuts (see below)

⅛ teaspoon coarsely ground pepper

Preheat the oven to 400 degrees F. Cut each pear half into ¼-inch-thick slices. Toss the pear slices with the Poire Williams and brown sugar in a large bowl.

Lay 1 sheet of phyllo dough flat on a clean work surface. Combine the melted butter with the walnut oil. Brush the phyllo lightly with the mixture, working from the edges towards the center. Layer the remaining 6 sheets of phyllo dough over the first, brushing each one with the butter mixture.

Layer the pear slices down the long edge of the phyllo, about 2 inches from the bottom edge and 1 inch in from each side. Cover the pears with the Gorgonzola cheese and toasted walnuts. Sprinkle with ground pepper. Fold the 2-inch flap of phyllo carefully over the filling and fold the sides over this. Roll the strudel up as

you would a jelly roll, as tightly as possible. Brush it with the butter mixture and place it seam-side down on an ungreased baking sheet.

Bake, 20 to 25 minutes, or until the strudel is golden and a skewer can be easily inserted into the center. Remove the strudel from the oven and let it rest for 5 minutes. Using a serrated knife, slice into 12 to 15 pieces.

To Toast Walnuts

Preheat the oven to 350 degrees F. Place coarsely chopped walnuts in a single layer on an ungreased baking sheet. Place in the oven and toast for 5 to 7 minutes, or until fragrant. Shake the pan occasionally while toasting to avoid burning or scorching the nuts.

Phyllo Spirals with Parmesan and Black Forest Ham

Makes 24 spirals

These tasty appetizers can be sliced and baked ahead of time and reheated right before serving.

6 sheets phyllo dough
6 tablespoons butter, melted
1 cup shredded Gruyère cheese

1 cup grated Parmesan cheese
6 to 8 ounces (6 to 8 slices) very thinly
   sliced Black Forest Ham

Lay 1 sheet of phyllo dough flat on a clean work surface. Lightly butter the phyllo, working from the edges towards the center. Lay a second sheet of phyllo over the first and butter it lightly.

Toss the Parmesan and Gruyère cheeses together. Sprinkle ¼ cup of the mixed cheeses over the buttered phyllo. Lay a third sheet of phyllo over the cheese and butter it lightly. Sprinkle another ¼ cup of the cheese over the phyllo. Layer the sliced ham over the cheese, covering the entire surface in a single layer. Lay a fourth sheet of phyllo over the ham and butter it lightly. Sprinkle the sheet of phyllo with ¼ cup of the cheese. Layer the remaining 2 sheets of phyllo over the fourth, buttering each one and sprinkling each with ¼ cup of the cheese.

Starting from the short end of the phyllo, start rolling up the layered sheets like a jelly roll. Be careful to roll the phyllo up as firmly and tightly as possible, without tearing the phyllo.

When the phyllo is completely rolled up, brush it liberally with butter and sprinkle the roll with the remaining shredded cheese. Wrap the roll in plastic wrap and refrigerate for at least 15 minutes to harden the butter.

Preheat the oven to 400 degrees F. Line a baking sheet with parchment paper. Using a serrated knife, slice the roll into twenty-four ½-inch-thick rounds. Place the slices in a single layer on the baking sheet. Bake for 7 to 10 minutes. Remove from the oven and turn the phyllo spirals over with a spatula. Return to the oven to bake for an additional 7 to 10 minutes, or until both sides of the spiral are crisp and golden. Serve warm.

Phyllo-Wrapped Lamb Wellington with Mint and Hazelnut Pesto

Makes 8 servings

In this elegant and appealing entrée, boneless lamb loin is slathered with a garlicky mint pesto and wrapped in a crackling, buttery phyllo crust. (Ask your butcher to bone and trim a saddle of lamb, which yields 2 lamb loins.) Serve with roasted new potatoes and steamed haricots verts for an easy, yet impressive, dinner.

For the mint and hazelnut pesto
3 cloves garlic
1 teaspoon salt
1 cup toasted and skinned hazelnuts (see below)
¼ cup hazelnut oil
⅓ cup vegetable oil
¼ cup fresh orange juice
1 teaspoon sugar
3 cups fresh mint leaves
1 cup fresh parsley sprigs

2 boneless lamb loins, about 1 pound each,
   trimmed of fat
2 tablespoons olive oil
Salt and pepper to taste
20 sheets phyllo dough
¾ cups (1 ½ sticks) butter, melted
8 sprigs fresh mint for garnish

To prepare the pesto, crush the garlic to a paste with the salt. Combine the garlic mixture, hazelnuts, oils, orange juice, and sugar in a blender or food processor. Puree the mixture until it is smooth but still has texture, about 30 seconds. Add the mint and parsley and process again until the mixture is combined.

Spread 2 tablespoons of the pesto over each lamb loin and wrap in plastic wrap. Allow the lamb to marinate in the refrigerator for 2 to 6 hours. Remove the lamb from the refrigerator and allow it to come to room temperature before searing.

Preheat the oven to 400 degrees F. In a large sauté pan or skillet, heat the olive oil over medium-high heat. Sear the lamb loins on all sides in the hot oil until they are brown but still raw inside, about 5 minutes. Remove the meat from the pan and allow it to cool. Season to taste with salt and pepper.

Lay 1 sheet of phyllo dough flat on a clean work surface. Lightly butter the phyllo, working from the edges towards the center. Layer 9 more sheets of phyllo over the first, buttering each one.

With the short edge of the phyllo facing you, spread 3 or 4 tablespoons of the mint pesto along this edge of the phyllo, about 2 inches from the bottom and 1 inch in from each side. Place one of the seared lamb loins over the pesto. Spread another 3 tablespoons of the pesto over the meat. Fold the 2-inch flap of phyllo over the meat and fold the 1-inch side flaps over it. Roll the lamb up in the phyllo as if it were a jelly roll, as tightly as possible. Brush the entire surface with melted butter and place it seam-side down on an ungreased baking sheet. Repeat this process with the remaining phyllo dough, lamb loin, and mint pesto.

Bake the lamb for 20 to 25 minutes, or until the phyllo is crusty and the lamb is medium rare.

Transfer the lamb to a cutting board and allow it to rest, loosely covered with foil, for about 5 minutes before slicing it. Using a sharp, serrated knife, slice each lamb loin into 6 to 8 pieces. Place 2 pieces of lamb on each serving plate and spoon an additional dollop of mint pesto onto each plate. Garnish with a sprig of fresh mint and serve.

To Toast and Skin Hazelnuts

Toast the nuts on a baking sheet in a 350-degree oven for about 10 to 15 minutes, or until they turn brown and fragrant and the skins start to look papery and peel away. Remove the nuts from the oven. Wrap the nuts in a rough towel, and scrub the skins off by rubbing them together firmly in the towel. Some of the skin may remain on the nut, but this won't affect the taste.

Brie and Lingonberry Puff

Makes 4 to 6 appetizer servings

This beautiful and impressive appetizer is the perfect beginning to a small, elegant dinner party. The golden mound of crisp phyllo hides a molten center of buttery melted Brie accented with tangy lingonberry preserves. Present it on a small, ornate platter in all its crusty splendor before slicing it for your guests.

One 8-ounce round Brie cheese
3 tablespoons lingonberry preserves

6 sheets phyllo dough
5 tablespoons butter, melted

Preheat the oven to 375 degrees F. Line a baking sheet with parchment paper.

Using a small sharp knife, carefully remove the rind around the sides of the cheese, leaving the rind on the top and bottom intact.

Slice the Brie in half, creating 2 circles of cheese. Spoon the lingonberry preserves over one half of the cheese and top with the remaining cheese half, making sure the rind is facing out.

Lay 1 sheet of phyllo dough flat on a clean work surface. Lightly butter the phyllo, working from the edges towards the center. Lay a second sheet of phyllo over the first and butter it lightly. Place the Brie in the center of the phyllo. With the short side facing you, bring the bottom part of the phyllo up and over the Brie, gently pressing it around the cheese. Bring the top flap of the phyllo down over the Brie and press it gently around the cheese as well. Wrap the side flaps of the phyllo up and fold over the top of the Brie, pressing

one and then the other side gently but firmly to fit the contours of the cheese. Lightly butter any dry phyllo. Set aside.

Lay a third sheet of phyllo vertically on a flat work surface and butter it. Lightly butter the fourth sheet of phyllo and lay it directly over the third sheet. Lightly butter and place a fifth sheet of phyllo horizontally over the fourth sheet. Lightly butter it and place the sixth and final sheet of phyllo over the fifth sheet. Place the phyllo-wrapped Brie in the center of these 4 sheets.

Carefully draw the phyllo up and around the Brie to form a pouch-shaped package, scrunching the last 2 or 3 inches of each sheet on top of the cheese to form a decorative topknot. Lightly butter the phyllo, pressing any loose phyllo gently against the sides of the Brie but leaving the top loose and crumbly looking. Drizzle any remaining butter over the phyllo topknot. Refrigerate the Brie puff for at least 15 minutes or up to 6 hours to harden the butter coating before baking.

Place the Brie puff on the prepared baking sheet and bake for 25 to 30 minutes, or until the phyllo is crisp and golden. Should the topknot start to brown too quickly, cover it lightly with a small piece of aluminum foil and continue baking.

Transfer the Brie puff to a wire rack and let cool for about 5 minutes. Present the pastry whole before slicing it with a serrated knife. Serve warm.

Malaysian Curried Shrimp with Snow Peas and Fresh Mango

Makes 4 servings

My husband tasted a wonderful dish in Malaysia that combined shrimp with snow peas, chunks of fresh mango, and a tangy curry sauce. This is my version of what he described, nestled on steamed rice in a delicate phyllo nest. This recipe will work for a first course or light entrée, depending on the appetite of the diner.

1 cup cooked white rice

4 standard-sized phyllo cups (see page 13)

2 tablespoons fresh yuzu juice (see note)
   or lime juice

2 teaspoons sugar

1 ½ tablespoons soy sauce

1 teaspoon Chinese chili-garlic paste

4 tablespoons vegetable oil

8 ounces fresh snow peas, julienned

Salt and pepper to taste

2 tablespoons mild curry paste

3 cloves garlic, minced

2 tablespoons minced fresh ginger

1 pound fresh medium shrimp, peeled
   and deveined

1 heaping cup cubed fresh mango

4 teaspoons chopped salted cashews

4 sprigs fresh cilantro, for garnish

Spoon ¼ cup of the white rice into each phyllo cup and place them in a 250-degree oven to keep warm.

In a small bowl, combine the yuzu or lime juice with the sugar, soy sauce, and chili paste. Stir to dissolve the sugar.

In a small nonstick sauté pan or skillet, heat 1 tablespoon of the oil and cook the snow peas over high heat for 1 to 1 ½ minutes until they are bright green and tender but still crisp. Season with salt and pepper. Set aside.

Heat the remaining 3 tablespoons oil in a large nonstick sauté pan or skillet over medium heat and sauté the curry paste, garlic, and ginger until fragrant, about 2 minutes.

Add the shrimp to the pan and cook just until they turn pink, 2 minutes. Stir in the yuzu or lime juice mixture and the snow peas. Toss to combine.

Remove the mixture from the heat and divide it among the 4 phyllo cups. Top each cup with one-fourth of the mango. Sprinkle each cup with 1 teaspoon chopped cashews and garnish with a sprig of cilantro. Serve immediately.

Note

A yuzu is a small Japanese citrus fruit that looks like a yellow tangerine. It is incredibly tangy and delicious; as strong as a lemon with a slight orange flavor.

Goat Cheese and Sweet Corn Tartlets

Makes 8 tartlets

Prepare these tartlets when the farmers' markets are bursting with fresh sweet corn. The pungent flavor and creamy texture of goat cheese adds a touch of luxurious richness. Serve with a spinach and watercress salad, or try the puckery sharpness of arugula as an alternative.

10 sheets phyllo dough
½ cup (1 stick) butter, melted,
   plus 1 tablespoon butter
2 cups sliced red onions

1 teaspoon sugar
8 ounces fresh white goat cheese, crumbled
1 cup cooked fresh corn kernels (2 ears)
Freshly ground pepper to taste

Lay 1 sheet of phyllo flat on a clean work surface. Lightly butter the phyllo, working from the edges towards the center. Layer 4 more sheets over the first, buttering each one.

Cut the layered phyllo into four 6-by 8-inch rectangles. Repeat this process with the remaining 5 sheets of phyllo to create a total of 8 rectangles.

To create a tartlet shell, take one phyllo rectangle and fold each side over by ½ inch. Fold each side over 2 more times, in ½-inch increments, to create a rectangular tartlet shell that is 3 ½ by 4 ½ inches. With your forefinger, gently compress each corner of the tartlet shell to prevent the rim from unraveling when it is baked. Lightly butter the completed shell and prick the bottom of the shell a few times with a fork. Repeat this process with the remaining phyllo rectangles. Chill the tartlet shells until ready to assemble.

In a small nonstick sauté pan or skillet, melt the 1 tablespoon butter. Cook the onions in the butter over medium heat until they begin to soften and are starting to brown lightly, 3 to 4 minutes. Sprinkle with the sugar and continue cooking until the onions are very soft and lightly caramelized, 2 or 3 minutes. Remove the pan from the heat and let cool completely.

Preheat the oven to 375 degrees F. To assemble, top each tartlet with some of the caramelized onions. Top the onions with 2 tablespoons of the corn kernels and 2 tablespoons of the goat cheese. Sprinkle a touch of pepper over the cheese.

Bake the tartlets on an ungreased baking sheet for 12 to 15 minutes, or until the phyllo is crisp and golden and the filling is hot. Serve immediately.

Wild Mushroom Strudel

Makes 6 to 8 servings

The buttery flavor of chanterelles is especially good in this strudel, along with a mixture of porcini, shiitake, portobello, and cremini mushrooms. Serve slices of this pastry as an appetizer or as an accompaniment to a simple grilled steak.

1 ounce dried porcini mushrooms
1 cup boiling water
2 tablespoons olive oil
¾ cup sliced shallots
2 cloves garlic, minced
1 ½ pounds mixed fresh mushrooms (chanterelle, shiitake, portobello, cremini, and oyster mushrooms) cleaned and sliced
3 tablespoons minced fresh thyme, or 1 tablespoon dried thyme

⅓ cup dry marsala
½ cup crème fraîche or sour cream
¼ cup chopped fresh Italian parsley
¼ cup grated Parmesan cheese
1 cup shredded Italian fontina cheese
Salt and pepper to taste
8 sheets phyllo dough
6 tablespoons (¾ stick) butter, melted

Place the dried mushrooms in a medium bowl and cover with the water. Let the mushrooms soak until the water is tepid. Remove the mushrooms from the water, squeezing any liquid from them back into the bowl, and coarsely chop them.

Slowly pour the mushroom soaking liquid through a coffee filter or a sieve lined with double-thickness paper towels into a small saucepan, removing any sediment. Bring the mushroom liquid to a boil over medium heat and cook to reduce by half. Remove from the heat and set aside to cool.

Preheat the oven to 400 degrees F. In a large sauté pan or skillet, heat the olive oil over medium-high heat. Add the shallots and cook until they are limp and just starting to brown, 2 to 3 minutes. Add the chopped garlic and continue cooking, stirring constantly, until the garlic is fragrant but not brown, 1 or 2 minutes more. Add the fresh mushrooms, porcini mushrooms, and thyme to the pan and cook over high heat until the mushrooms are tender.

Add the marsala, stir to scrape the browned bits from the bottom of the pan, and cook until most of the liquid is evaporated. Add the mushroom liquid to the mixture and continue cooking until it, too, is evaporated. Remove the mushrooms from the heat and allow them to cool completely.

When the mushrooms are cool, stir in the crème fraîche or sour cream, parsley, and cheeses. Season with salt and pepper and refrigerate.

Lay 1 sheet of phyllo dough flat on a clean work surface. Lightly butter the phyllo, working from the edges towards the center. Layer the remaining 7 sheets of phyllo over the first, buttering each one.

Spread the cool filling down the long side of the phyllo, about 2 inches from the bottom and 1 inch in from each side. Fold the bottom edge and sides over the filling and roll the pastry up like a jelly roll. Place the strudel, seam-side down, on an ungreased baking sheet, and lightly brush the top and sides of the strudel with any remaining melted butter.

Bake for 20 to 25 minutes, or until the pastry is crisp and golden and the filling is hot. Remove the strudel from the oven and let it rest for about 5 minutes. Slice into diagonal pieces using a serrated knife. Serve immediately.

Phyllo Pouches with Poached Chicken and Herbed Mustard Sauce

Makes 6 pouches

This is a wonderful buffet dish, as the pouches can be prepared in advance and look gorgeous grouped together on a large silver platter. To prevent the pouches from blossoming open in the oven and spilling their contents before they are presented, tie cotton string around their necks. Snip the string and remove it before serving the pouch.

2 tablespoons olive oil

2 cups sliced leeks (white portion only)

½ cup Champagne or dry white wine

2 cups heavy cream

⅓ cup grainy mustard

2 tablespoons chopped fresh tarragon leaves

Salt and pepper to taste

6 boneless, skinless chicken breasts (about
 1 ¼ pounds) poached and chilled

18 sheets phyllo dough

¾ cup (1 ½ sticks) butter, melted

1 ¼ cups toasted bread crumbs

Preheat the oven to 375 degrees F.

In a large sauté pan or skillet, heat the olive oil and sauté the leeks over medium-high heat until they are limp and golden, 4 to 5 minutes. Increase the heat to high and add the Champagne or white wine. Stir to scrape up any browned bits from the bottom of the pan. Cook until the liquid is almost completely evaporated, 3 to 4 minutes.

Add the cream and reduce the heat to medium low. Simmer the sauce until it thickens, 15 to 20 minutes. Stir in the mustard and the tarragon and season with salt and pepper. Allow the sauce to cool, then cover and refrigerate for at least 1 hour. Coarsely shred the chicken and stir it into the cream sauce. Set aside.

Lay 1 sheet of phyllo dough flat on a clean work surface. Lightly butter the phyllo, working from the outer edges towards the center. Sprinkle with 1 tablespoon of the toasted bread crumbs. Layer 5 more sheets of phyllo over the first, buttering each one and sprinkling each sheet with 1 tablespoon of the toasted bread crumbs.

Using an 8-inch round cake pan as a template, cut two 8-inch circles from the layered pastry dough. Spoon about ⅓ cup of the cold chicken filling into the center of each phyllo circle. Gather the phyllo up around the filling and form into a pouch, or "beggar's purse," shape. Pinch the neck closed and tie it loosely with a piece of cotton string. Repeat this process with the remaining phyllo and chicken filling. You should end up with a total of 6 pouches.

Brush the finished pouches with the remaining melted butter and refrigerate until the butter coating is firm, about 30 minutes. (The pouches can be refrigerated up to 24 hours.)

Preheat the oven to 375 degrees F. Place all 6 pouches on an ungreased baking sheet and bake for 25 to 30 minutes, or until the pastry is crisp and golden and the filling is hot. Remove the pouches from the oven, clip and remove the string, and serve immediately.

Miniature Moussaka Nests

Makes 24 nests

These tiny, elegant mouthfuls are packed with a lively combination of flavors that will transport your taste buds to a sunny taverna on the coast of Corfu. Surprisingly satisfying, one or two of these tidbits will appease the most ravenous appetite.

8 small red potatoes (1 ½ to 2 inches in diameter)

1 small Japanese eggplant (6 to 8 ounces), diced

1 tablespoon olive oil

8 ounces ground lamb

Salt and pepper to taste

1 clove garlic, crushed

¼ cup dry sherry

1 tablespoon tomato paste

⅛ teaspoon ground cinnamon

½ teaspoon ground cumin

2 tablespoons chopped fresh mint

6 sheets phyllo dough

5 tablespoons butter, melted

Béchamel Sauce (recipe follows)

½ cup grated Parmesan cheese

Cover the potatoes with cold salted water in a medium saucepan and bring to a boil over high heat. Reduce the heat to medium low and cook the potatoes until tender, 8 to 10 minutes. Drain and cool completely.

In a large sauté pan or skillet over medium-high heat, sauté the eggplant in the olive oil until it starts to soften. Add the lamb and season with salt and pepper. Continue cooking until the lamb is brown and crumbly and the eggplant is very tender, 7 to 10 minutes. Drain the lamb well on a plate lined with paper towels. Return the lamb and eggplant mixture to the pan and add the garlic, sherry, tomato paste, spices, and mint. Cook over low heat for about 10 minutes to allow the flavors to combine. Adjust the seasoning and let cool completely.

Preheat the oven to 375 degrees F. Spray two 12-cup miniature muffin tins with a vegetable-oil spray.

Lay 1 sheet of phyllo dough flat on a clean work surface. Lightly butter the phyllo, working from the edges towards the center. Layer 2 more sheets of phyllo over the first, lightly buttering each one. Using a ruler as a guide, cut the phyllo into twelve 3-inch squares. Press 1 square into each muffin cup. Repeat this process with the remaining 3 sheets of phyllo dough and the second muffin tin.

To assemble the moussaka nests, slice the cooled potatoes into ⅛-inch-thick slices. Spoon 1 heaping teaspoon of the cooled lamb mixture into each of the unbaked phyllo nests. Top with a slice of potato. Spoon 1 teaspoon of the béchamel sauce on top of the potato slices and sprinkle each nest with 1 teaspoon of the Parmesan cheese.

Bake the pastries for 12 to 15 minutes, or until they are golden and the béchamel sauce is puffy and lightly browned.

Béchamel Sauce

Makes 1 cup

Infusing milk with a mixture of spices and aromatic vegetables gives this subtle, creamy sauce a more complex flavor. The process isn't difficult and the ingredients are pantry staples. If you don't have all the flavor infusions, even three or four of them will enhance the taste of the sauce.

1 cup milk
1 bay leaf
4 peppercorns
1 sliver onion
1 sliver carrot
1 sliver celery

1 mushroom
1 sprig fresh parsley
2 tablespoons butter
2 tablespoons flour
⅛ teaspoon ground or freshly grated nutmeg
Salt and pepper to taste

In a medium saucepan, combine the milk with the bay leaf, peppercorns, onion, carrot, celery, mushroom, and parsley. Warm the milk over medium heat until bubbles form around the edge. Remove the pan from the heat and cover it to allow the flavors to infuse into the milk, at least 15 minutes.

In another medium saucepan, melt the butter over medium-high heat. Add the flour and cook, stirring constantly, until the roux is a light brown toasty color, 1 to 2 minutes. Strain the warm milk into the roux and whisk constantly over medium heat until it is thickened. Bring the mixture to a boil and cook for 1 minute. (This will remove any flour taste from the sauce.)

Remove the pan from the heat, add the nutmeg, and season with salt and pepper. Let cool completely.

Note

The miniature moussaka nests can be frozen for up to 1 month before they are baked. Bake the frozen pastries directly from the freezer without thawing them first. They may take 1 or 2 minutes longer to cook when frozen.

Caribbean Crème Brûlée with Coconut Phyllo Twists

Makes 6 custards and 12 twists

Restaurant chefs give their crème brûlée a brittle sugar crust with a quick blast from a small propane blowtorch (available at most hardware stores). Feeling too timid for this method? A very hot broiler will work as well. Crunchy coconut phyllo cookies enhance the tropical mood of this voluptuous custard, which is subtly flavored with coconut cream and dark rum.

For the crème brûlée

1 tablespoon unsalted butter, melted
8 egg yolks
6 tablespoons granulated sugar
¼ cup coconut cream (see note)
2 cups heavy cream
3 tablespoons dark rum
Pinch of salt
¼ cup superfine sugar

For the coconut phyllo twists

2 sheets phyllo dough
2 tablespoons unsalted butter, melted
3 to 5 tablespoons granulated sugar
3 tablespoons flaked coconut

To prepare the custard, preheat the oven to 275 degrees F. Brush six 6-ounce ceramic ramekins with the melted butter. Place the ramekins in a 13-by-9-by-2-inch baking pan.

In a large bowl, whisk the egg yolks, granulated sugar, and coconut cream together until smooth. Stir in the heavy cream, rum, and salt. Strain the custard through a fine sieve. Carefully pour ¾ cup of the mixture into each ramekin.

Pour enough warm water into the baking pan to come halfway up the sides of the ramekins. Place the pan on the middle rack of the oven and bake until the custard is set but still slightly wobbly in the very center, 45 to 50 minutes.

Remove the ramekins from the pan and let cool to room temperature. Cover with plastic wrap and refrigerate until very cold, 6 to 8 hours.

No more than 1 hour before serving, sprinkle each custard with 2 teaspoons of the superfine sugar. Flatten the sugar with the back of a teaspoon. Caramelize the sugar with a quick blast from a propane blowtorch, or preheat the broiler, return the ramekins to the baking dish, surround them with ice cubes, and place the custards under the broiler for about 2 minutes. The sugar will melt, bubble, and turn a golden brown, then become crisp as it cools. Refrigerate the custards until ready to serve.

To prepare the twists, preheat the oven to 375 degrees F. Line a baking sheet with parchment paper.

Lay 1 sheet of phyllo dough flat on a clean work surface. Lightly butter the phyllo, working from the edges to the center. Sprinkle with 1 to 2 tablespoons of the granulated sugar and 2 tablespoons of the coconut. Top with the second sheet of phyllo dough. Lightly butter the second sheet and sprinkle with 1 or 2 tablespoons of sugar.

Cut the phyllo into twelve 3-by-3-inch squares, discarding any scraps. Turn 1 square so that it looks like a diamond. Starting from the bottom point of the diamond, roll up the phyllo, twisting and compressing it into a log shape. Repeat this with the remaining phyllo squares.

Place the twists on the prepared baking sheet and brush them lightly with some butter. Sprinkle with the remaining 1 tablespoon sugar and the remaining 1 tablespoon coconut.

Bake the cookies for 7 to 9 minutes, or until they are crisp, golden, and lightly caramelized. Transfer to wire racks to cool completely. Serve with the chilled custards.

Note

I like the Coco Lopez brand of coconut cream, which is often used for piña coladas and other tropical drinks.

Baklava

This traditional Greek sweet remains as popular as it is delicious. Enjoy it as they do in Greece, as an afternoon snack accompanied with a sweet iced coffee.

For the pastry

1 ½ cups finely chopped walnuts
1 cup finely chopped almonds
⅓ cup granulated sugar
1 teaspoon ground cinnamon
¼ teaspoon ground cardamom
⅛ teaspoon ground cloves

16 sheets phyllo dough
¾ cup (1 ½ sticks) unsalted butter, melted

For the syrup

1 cup granulated sugar
1 cup water
1 cup honey
One 3-inch strip lemon peel
½ vanilla bean, halved lengthwise
1 cinnamon stick

To prepare the pastry, preheat the oven to 350 degrees F. Lightly butter the bottom and sides of a 9-by-13-by-2-inch pan with melted butter or spray with a vegetable-oil spray.

In a small bowl, combine the walnuts, almonds, granulated sugar, cinnamon, cardamom, and cloves. Set aside.

Using the bottom of the prepared pan as a template, cut the phyllo dough to fit the pan, discarding any scraps. Place 1 sheet of phyllo in the pan and lightly brush it with butter. Layer 3 more sheets of phyllo over the first, buttering each one. Sprinkle one third of the nut mixture over the dough. Layer 4 more sheets of phyllo over the nut mixture, buttering each one. Sprinkle with one third of the nut mixture. Layer 4 more sheets of phyllo over the second layer of nuts, buttering each one. Sprinkle with the final one third of the nut mixture. Finally, layer 8 more sheets of phyllo over the nuts, buttering each one.

Using a sharp knife, score the baklava into diamond-shaped pieces by cutting through just the top layers of phyllo dough. Bake the baklava in the oven until it is crisp and brown, 45 to 60 minutes.

Meanwhile, prepare the honey syrup: combine all the ingredients in a large saucepan. Bring the syrup to a boil over medium-high heat. Reduce the heat to low and simmer the syrup until it is the consistency of thick maple syrup, about 10 minutes. Remove the syrup from the heat and let cool slightly.

As soon as the baklava comes out of the oven, pour the still-warm syrup over it.

Let the baklava cool completely. It may be served at room temperature or chilled. To store, lightly cover the baklava and refrigerate for up to 4 days.

Venetian Napoleons

Makes 8 napoleons

Layers of almond-scented phyllo cut into irregular triangles, like shards of glass, distinguish this lovely pastry. Mascarpone cheese and juicy strawberries marinated in a piquant mixture of port and balsamic vinegar resonate with the flavors of Italy.

6 sheets phyllo dough

6 tablespoons (¾ stick) unsalted
   butter, melted

6 tablespoons ground almonds

6 tablespoons raw or granulated sugar,
   plus more for garnish (optional)

2 cups (1 pound) mascarpone cheese
   at room temperature

½ cup packed light brown sugar

½ teaspoon vanilla extract

4 cups sliced strawberries

1 tablespoon balsamic vinegar

2 tablespoons port

Preheat the oven to 375 degrees F. Line a baking sheet with parchment paper.

Lay 1 sheet of phyllo dough flat on a clean work surface. Lightly butter the phyllo, working from the edges towards the center. Sprinkle the phyllo with 1 tablespoon of the ground almonds and 1 tablespoon of the sugar. Layer the remaining 5 sheets of phyllo over the first, buttering and sprinkling each one.

With a sharp knife, cut the phyllo into 24 irregularly shaped triangles. Using a large metal spatula, carefully place the phyllo triangles on the prepared baking sheet. Bake them until they are crisp and golden, 5 to 7 minutes. Transfer the phyllo triangles to wire racks to cool completely.

In a medium bowl, stir the mascarpone cheese, ¼ cup of the light brown sugar, and the vanilla extract until smooth. Cover and refrigerate until ready to serve.

No more than 30 minutes before serving, toss the sliced strawberries, the remaining ¼ cup brown sugar, the balsamic vinegar, and port together in a separate bowl.

To serve, place 1 phyllo triangle on a dessert plate and top with 2 heaping tablespoons of the cheese mixture. Spoon ¼ cup of the marinated berries over the mascarpone. Place a second phyllo triangle over the berries, but do not attempt to line it up exactly with the first triangle. Top the second phyllo triangle with another 2 heaping tablespoons of the cheese mixture and another ¼ cup of strawberries. Top with a third phyllo triangle. Sprinkle some raw or granulated sugar around the pastry on the dessert plate to garnish, if desired, and serve. Repeat the process for the other 7 portions.

Linzer Tarts

These jewel-like tarts are distinguished by the classic mixture of hazelnuts and raspberries and a rich, gooey texture reminiscent of pecan pie.

¼ cup corn syrup
¼ cup packed light brown sugar
Pinch of salt
½ cup plus 2 tablespoons (1 ¼ sticks)
   unsalted butter, melted
1 egg

1 teaspoon vanilla extract
¾ cup hazelnuts, toasted and skinned
   (see page 37)
12 sheets phyllo dough
¼ cup raspberry jam
Confectioners' sugar for sprinkling

In a small bowl, whisk together the corn syrup, brown sugar, salt, 2 tablespoons of the melted butter, the egg, and vanilla until smooth. Stir in the hazelnuts and set aside.

Preheat the oven to 375 degrees F. Spray two 12-cup miniature muffin tins with a vegetable-oil spray.

Lay 1 sheet of phyllo dough flat on a clean work surface. Lightly butter the phyllo, working from the edges towards the center. Layer 5 more sheets of phyllo over the first, buttering each one. Using a ruler as a guide, cut the phyllo into twelve 3-inch squares. Press 1 square into each cup in the first muffin tin. Repeat this process with the remaining 6 sheets of phyllo and the second muffin tin.

Spoon ½ teaspoon of the raspberry jam into each phyllo cup. Spoon 1 or 2 tablespoons of the hazelnut

mixture over the jam, giving each cup at least 4 whole hazelnuts.

Bake the tarts for 15 to 18 minutes, or until the phyllo is crisp and golden and the hazelnut filling is set. Transfer the tins to a wire rack to cool before removing the tarts from the muffin tins. Sprinkle with confectioners' sugar before serving.

Caramelized Apple Napoleons

Makes 6 napoleons

This spectacular alternative to apple pie is a real showstopper. Crispy layers of phyllo sprinkled with cinnamon and sugar and dusted with ground pecans encase a filling of brandied caramel cream and caramelized apples. Although the recipe consists of several components, they are not difficult to prepare, and some can be made in advance. Dark rum or bourbon can be substituted for the brandy, if you prefer.

For the brandied caramel cream

2 cups heavy cream

1 cup granulated sugar

⅓ cup brandy

For the pastry

¾ cup granulated sugar

2 teaspoons ground cinnamon

6 sheets phyllo dough

5 tablespoons butter, melted

6 tablespoons ground pecans

For the caramelized apples

6 medium Fuji or Golden Delicious apples

¾ cup granulated sugar

4 tablespoons melted butter

Confectioners' sugar for sprinkling

To prepare the brandied caramel cream, warm ½ cup of the cream in a small saucepan over low heat. Set aside and keep warm. Combine the sugar and brandy in a medium, heavy saucepan. Without stirring, cook over low heat until the sugar dissolves. Increase the heat to high and boil the syrup until it is golden in color and slightly thickened, about 3 to 5 minutes. Do not leave the syrup unattended, as it can get too dark and burn quickly.

Remove the caramel syrup from the heat and stir in the warmed cream. (Be careful not to let the hot caramel splatter on you, as the sauce may bubble ferociously when the cream is added.)

When the sauce is smooth, stir in the remaining 1 ½ cups cream. Continue stirring until the caramel sauce is completely combined with the cream. Pour the caramel cream into a heatproof bowl, cover, and refrigerate until very cold, 4 to 8 hours.

Using an electric mixer set at medium-high speed, whip the caramel cream until it holds soft peaks. Increase the mixer speed to high and continue beating until the cream is thick and holds stiff peaks. Cover and refrigerate up to 2 hours before serving.

To prepare the pastry, preheat the oven to 375 degrees F. Line a baking sheet with parchment paper. In a small bowl, stir together the sugar and cinnamon.

Lay 1 sheet of phyllo dough flat on a clean work surface. Lightly butter the phyllo, working from the edges towards the center. Sprinkle with 2 tablespoons of the cinnamon sugar and 1 tablespoon of the ground pecans. Layer the remaining 5 sheets of phyllo dough over the first, buttering and sprinkling each one with the cinnamon sugar and nuts. With a sharp knife, cut the layered phyllo into four 3-by-17 ½-inch strips. Cut each strip into three 5 ½-inch pieces, discarding any scraps. This should yield twelve 3-by-5 ½-inch rectangles.

Using a large spatula, carefully place the phyllo rectangles on the prepared baking sheet and bake for 6 to 10 minutes, or until the phyllo is crisp, golden, and lightly caramelized. Transfer to wire racks and let cool. The phyllo will become crisper as it cools. The pastries can be prepared 1 day in advance and stored in an airtight container to retain their crispness.

To prepare the caramelized apples, peel, core, and slice each apple into 8 wedges. Coat each apple wedge well in the sugar.

In a large nonstick sauté pan skillet, melt the butter over medium-high heat. Place the apples in a single layer in the pan and cook them until they are golden and caramelized, 3 to 5 minutes. Turn over the apple slices and cook them until they are tender and caramelized on the other side, another 3 to 5 minutes. Remove the pan from the heat, cover, and keep warm. (If all the apple wedges cannot be cooked in a single layer, cook them in 2 batches, using half of the butter for each batch.)

To serve, place 1 phyllo rectangle on a dessert plate. Top the pastry with 8 apple wedges and drizzle with a little bit of the syrup from the cooked apples. Top with ½ cup of the cream. Place a second pastry rectangle on top of the cream and sprinkle with some confectioners' sugar. Repeat the process for the remaining 5 portions. Serve immediately.

Rhubarb Crumble with Candied Ginger Crème Anglaise

Makes 6 servings

I love rhubarb, with its robust tang and brilliant rosy hue. The flavor of this warm fruit compote, contrasted with a sweet yet spicy crème anglaise, is sublime, and the phyllo crumble is as easy to make as crumpling up a piece of paper. The crème anglaise and phyllo crumbles can be prepared separately up to 2 days ahead of time.

For the ginger crème anglaise

3 cups half-and-half

¾ cup granulated sugar

One 3-inch piece fresh ginger, peeled
  and sliced

7 egg yolks, well beaten

1 tablespoon ginger liqueur (optional)

¼ cup finely diced candied ginger

For the phyllo crumbles

6 sheets phyllo dough

5 tablespoons unsalted butter

Granulated sugar for sprinkling

For the rhubarb

2 pounds fresh rhubarb, cut into 1 ½- to
  2-inch pieces

1 teaspoon grated lemon zest

1 cup granulated sugar

2 tablespoons flour

⅛ teaspoon ground or freshly grated nutmeg

2 tablespoons unsalted butter

To prepare the crème anglaise, combine the half-and-half, sugar, and sliced ginger in a large, heavy-stainless steel saucepan (an aluminum pan will turn the custard gray). Stir over medium heat until the sugar is dissolved.

Stir ½ cup of the half-and-half mixture into the egg yolks. Stir this mixture into the half-and-half in the saucepan. Cook over very low heat, stirring constantly,

until the custard is thick enough to coat the back of a spoon, about 10 minutes. Do not allow the sauce to boil, or it will curdle. Strain the thickened custard through a sieve into a large bowl. Discard the fresh ginger. Allow the sauce to cool completely. Stir in the ginger liqueur, if using, and the candied ginger. Cover and refrigerate until thoroughly chilled.

To prepare the phyllo crumbles, preheat the oven to 350 degrees F. Line a baking sheet with parchment paper.

Lay 1 sheet of phyllo dough flat on a clean work surface. Lightly butter the phyllo, working from the edges towards the center. Crumple the phyllo into a loose ball, as you would crumple a piece of paper. Repeat this with the remaining phyllo. Place the phyllo crumbles on the baking sheet and sprinkle them liberally with sugar. Bake for 7 to 8 minutes, or until golden and crisp. Let cool completely before serving.

To prepare the rhubarb, preheat the oven to 350 degrees F. In a large bowl, combine the rhubarb with the lemon zest and ½ cup of the sugar. Let sit for about 20 minutes, or until the sugar begins to dissolve. In another small bowl, combine the remaining ½ cup sugar, the flour, and nutmeg. Toss the rhubarb with this mixture.

Butter a 9-by-9-by-2-inch baking pan with 1 tablespoon of the butter and spoon the rhubarb into it. Shave the remaining 1 tablespoon butter over the top of the fruit. Cover the pan with aluminum foil and bake until the rhubarb is tender but still holding its shape and the juices are thick and bubbly, about 30 minutes. Remove the pan from the oven and uncover the rhubarb. Let the fruit cool slightly before serving.

To serve, spoon ½ cup of the crème anglaise onto a dessert plate and top with ⅓ cup of the warm rhubarb. Top the rhubarb with a phyllo crumble. Repeat with the remaining 5 portions. Serve immediately.

Strudel of Winter Fruit Compote

Makes 8 to 10 servings

Reminiscent of Eastern European rugelach, this strudel is tangy and rich with a sweet, flaky crust. The compote is also excellent on its own or over ice cream.

For the compote

1 cup granulated sugar

1 cup water

½ vanilla bean, halved lengthwise

One 2-by-3-inch strip lemon zest
   (use vegetable peeler)

3 ounces dried Calimyrna figs

2 ounces dried pears

3 ounces dried peaches

3 ounces dried apricots

½ cup dried sour cherries

3 to 4 tablespoons dark rum

7 sheets phyllo dough

6 tablespoons unsalted butter, melted

¾ cup plus 2 tablespoons ground pistachio
   nuts or pecans

3 tablespoons granulated sugar

To prepare the fruit compote, combine the sugar and water in a large saucepan and stir constantly over medium heat until the sugar has dissolved. Scrape the seeds from the vanilla bean using the tip of a sharp knife and add them and the bean to the sugar syrup. Increase the heat to high and boil the syrup for 1 minute.

Remove the pan from the heat and add the lemon peel, figs, and pears. Cover and gently poach the fruit over medium-low heat for about 25 minutes. Add the peaches and continue poaching for 10 minutes. Stir in the apricots and the cherries and continue poaching for another 5 to 6 minutes. The fruit should be soft but retain its shape. Remove the pan from the heat. Allow the fruit to cool completely in its syrup, 30 to 60 minutes.

Transfer the fruit to a large crock or jar, leaving any syrup the fruit hasn't absorbed in the saucepan. Return the saucepan to the stove and cook over medium heat to reduce the syrup to the consistency of thick maple syrup. Stir in the rum. Pour the syrup over the fruit. Let cool completely, cover, and refrigerate for at least 1 to 2 hours. The compote can be made ahead and stored in the refrigerator for up to 1 week.

Preheat the oven to 375 degrees F. Line a baking sheet with parchment paper. Remove the fruit from the syrup, drain, and coarsely chop. Reserve about 2 tablespoons of the syrup.

Lay 1 sheet of phyllo dough flat on a clean work surface. Lightly butter the phyllo, working from the edges towards the center. Sprinkle with 2 tablespoons of the nuts. Layer the remaining 6 sheets of phyllo over the first, buttering and sprinkling each one with nuts. Spoon the fruit compote evenly down the long side of the phyllo, about 2 inches from the bottom edge and 1 inch in from both sides. Drizzle the filling with 1 or 2 tablespoons of the fruit syrup. Fold the bottom edge and the side flaps over the filling and roll up the phyllo like a jelly roll.

Brush the strudel lightly with melted butter and roll it in the sugar. Place the strudel, seam-side down, on the baking sheet. Bake for 25 to 30 minutes, or until crisp and golden.

Remove the strudel from the oven and let it rest for a few minutes before slicing. Slice on the diagonal with a serrated knife. Serve warm or at room temperature.

Phyllo Cannoli

Makes 8 cannoli

Sprinkling the phyllo dough with sugar will give these cannoli shells a sweet flavor and a crunchy texture that stands up well to the sturdy ricotta filling. However, if a more-delicate, less-sweet shell is desired, simply eliminate the granulated sugar when preparing the shells. Cannoli forms are available at specialty food shops and restaurant supply stores.

1 cup heavy cream
2 tablespoons Grand Marnier or other orange
   liqueur
1 cup confectioners' sugar, sifted
1 tablespoon frozen orange juice concentrate,
   thawed
Grated zest of 1 orange

6 ounces semisweet chocolate, finely chopped
1 cup whole or part-skim milk ricotta cheese
8 sheets phyllo dough
½ cup (1 stick) unsalted butter, melted
½ cup granulated sugar (optional)
¼ cup finely chopped pistachio nuts
Confectioners' sugar for sprinkling

Preheat the oven to 375 degrees F. Line a baking sheet with parchment paper.

In a large bowl, combine the cream, Grand Marnier or other liqueur, confectioners' sugar, and orange juice concentrate. Using an electric mixer set at medium speed, beat the cream until it holds soft peaks. Increase the speed to high and continue beating the cream until it is very thick and holds firm peaks.

Stir the orange zest, chocolate, and ricotta cheese together in a separate bowl. Fold the orange cream into the ricotta mixture until thoroughly combined. Cover and refrigerate.

Spray the cannoli forms with a vegetable-oil spray. Lay 1 sheet of phyllo dough flat on a clean work surface.

Lightly butter the phyllo working from the edges towards the center. Sprinkle the phyllo with 1 tablespoon of the granulated sugar, if using. Lay a second sheet of phyllo over the first, brush with butter and sprinkle with 1 tablespoon granulated sugar, if using. Cut the phyllo in half lengthwise to create two 6-by-17 ½-inch strips. Place the cannoli form at the bottom of one of these strips. Roll it up as tightly as possible without tearing the phyllo, brushing the dry phyllo lightly with butter as you do so. Brush the finished phyllo tube with butter and sprinkle with some more granulated sugar, if using. Repeat this process with another cannoli form and the second strip of phyllo. Prepare the remaining 6 cannoli shells as with the first two, using the remaining phyllo, butter, and optional sugar.

Place the cannoli shells, seam-side down, on the prepared baking sheet. Bake for 10 to 12 minutes, or until the phyllo is golden and the sugar is lightly caramelized. Remove the shells from the oven and let cool just until they can be handled. Carefully push each cannoli shell off the mold. (Do this gently so that you do not crush the phyllo.) Let the shells cool completely on a wire rack before filling.

Fill a large pastry bag with the ricotta filling. Do not fit the bag with a metal tip—the large opening of the pastry bag will allow the chocolate chunks to be piped out. Pipe the ricotta filling into the phyllo shells, leaving some of the filling extruding from each end. Dip each end in chopped pistachios. Sprinkle each cannoli with confectioners' sugar before serving.

Caramel-Pecan Slices

Makes 48 cookies

These cookies—really a cross between a cookie and a confection—are a little slice of heaven. Gooey, decadent, and addictive, a sliver goes a long way. This recipe makes a large quantity, perfect for gift giving.

¾ cup mild honey

2 cups heavy cream

2 ½ cups granulated sugar

⅛ teaspoon salt

2 teaspoons vanilla extract

12 ounces pecans, coarsely chopped

18 sheets phyllo dough

¾ cup (1 ½ sticks) unsalted butter, melted

In a 2-quart saucepan, bring the honey, cream, 1 ¼ cups of the sugar, and the salt to a boil over high heat. Cook, stirring occasionally, for about 5 minutes, or until the mixture becomes a thick syrup and registers 240 degrees F on a candy thermometer, or a small amount poured into a cup of cold water forms a soft, pliable ball. Remove the syrup from the heat and stir in the vanilla and the pecans.

Pour the caramel into an oiled medium-sized bowl and let it rest until it is cool enough to handle but still malleable. Divide the caramel into 6 equal portions. Using your hands, shape each portion into a long rope about 16 inches long and ¾ inch thick. Allow the caramel ropes to cool completely. They will firm up as they cool.

Preheat the oven to 375 degrees F. Line a baking sheet with parchment paper.

Lay 1 sheet of phyllo dough flat on a clean work surface. Lightly butter the phyllo, working from the edges towards the center. Sprinkle with 2 tablespoons of the remaining sugar. Layer 2 more sheets of phyllo over the first, buttering and sprinkling each one. Lay 1 caramel rope down the long side of the phyllo about 1 inch from the edge. Fold the 1-inch flap over the caramel and continue rolling it up as if it were a jelly roll. Brush the caramel roll with butter and sprinkle with sugar. Lay the roll, seam-side down, on the baking sheet. Pinch the ends of the pastry closed. Repeat this process with the remaining phyllo and the 5 caramel ropes, forming a total of 6 large rolls.

Bake the rolls on the prepared pan, 3 at a time, until the phyllo is golden and crisp, 15 to 20 minutes. Transfer the rolls to wire racks to cool completely, then cut each roll into 8 diagonal slices, 1 ½ to 2 inches long.

Fresh Blackberry Tart with Walnut Streusel and Crème Fraîche Ice Cream

Makes 6 servings

The casually crimped edges of the free-form tart shell give this berry pie its rustic charm. Dispense with worries about a tender crust, for the sweet phyllo shell remains flaky under its burden of fresh fruit. This tart is delicious served warm with a scoop of crème fraîche ice cream.

For the tart shell

8 sheets phyllo dough

½ cup (1 stick) unsalted butter, melted

½ cup granulated sugar

½ cup amaretti, gingersnap, or other crisp
    cookie crumbs

For the streusel

4 tablespoons (½ stick) chilled unsalted butter

½ cup all-purpose flour

½ cup granulated sugar, plus more for sprinkling

½ cup coarsely chopped toasted walnuts

For the filling

1 tablespoon fresh lemon juice

⅓ cup granulated sugar

2 tablespoons cornstarch

⅛ teaspoon ground or freshly grated nutmeg

3 cups fresh blackberries (see note)

Crème fraîche ice cream (recipe follows)

To prepare the tart shell, line a large baking sheet with parchment paper or aluminum foil. (A baking sheet without sides is best for this recipe.) Lay 1 sheet of phyllo dough lengthwise on the baking sheet. Lightly butter the phyllo, working from the edges towards the center. Sprinkle with 1 tablespoon of the sugar and 1 tablespoon of the cookie crumbs. (Butter each of the following sheets then sprinkle with sugar and crumbs after it is placed correctly.) Lay the second sheet of phyllo directly over the first. Lay the third sheet crosswise across the center of the first 2 sheets. Lay the fourth sheet of phyllo directly over the third. Lay the fifth sheet of phyllo diagonally over the stack. Lay the sixth sheet of phyllo on the stack, running it on the opposite diagonal so that the fifth and sixth sheets form an X. Lay the seventh sheet of phyllo in the same direction as the fifth sheet. Lay the eighth and final sheet of phyllo in the same direction as the sixth sheet and give the stack a final light buttering and sprinkling. The phyllo stack should now form a rough pastry circle.

Start rolling the outer edges of the phyllo circle towards the center, creating an 8-inch tart shell with a 1- to 1 ½-inch-high rim. Give the finished shell a final light buttering and generously sprinkle the bottom and rim of the shell with sugar. Refrigerate the shell to allow the butter to harden while you prepare the streusel and the fruit filling.

Preheat the oven to 400 degrees F. To prepare the streusel, combine the butter, flour, and sugar in a large bowl. Using your fingers, rub the ingredients together until the mixture is crumbly and the pieces of butter are no bigger than small peas. Chill the streusel until the butter is firm. This will prevent the streusel from melting into the fruit filling. Toss the chilled streusel with the walnuts.

To prepare the filling, stir together the lemon juice, sugar, cornstarch, and nutmeg in a small bowl. Toss the berries with the mixture and spoon into the tart shell. Top the berries with the walnut streusel.

Bake the tart until the berries are bubbling and the tart shell is crisp and golden brown, 25 to 30 minutes. If the phyllo shell seems to be browning too quickly, cover the rim with aluminum foil and continue baking until the filling is cooked through.

Transfer the tart to a wire rack to cool before cutting into wedges with a serrated knife. Serve wedges of the tart, warm, with a scoop of crème fraîche ice cream.

Note

You may substitute fresh, sliced peaches or nectarines, or fresh raspberries for the blackberries.

Crème Fraîche Ice Cream

Makes 1 quart

1 vanilla bean
2 cups whole or low-fat milk
4 large egg yolks

1 cup granulated sugar
2 cups crème fraîche

Split the vanilla bean lengthwise and, using the tip of a sharp knife, scrape out the seeds. In a large saucepan, combine the milk, vanilla seeds, and vanilla bean. Heat over medium-high heat until the mixture is warm and bubbles start to form around its edges. Remove from heat, cover, and allow the vanilla flavor to infuse the milk for at least 10 minutes. Remove the vanilla bean from the milk.

In a medium bowl, beat the egg yolks and sugar together until they are thick and the sugar is dissolved. Whisk about ½ cup of the warm milk into the egg yolks. Combine this mixture with the remaining milk in the saucepan and stir to combine. Return the saucepan to the stove and cook the mixture gently over low heat, stirring constantly until it is thick enough to coat the back of a spoon, 7 to 10 minutes. Do not allow the custard to boil, or it will curdle.

Strain the custard through a sieve into a clean bowl. Sprinkle the top of the custard with some sugar to prevent a skin from forming as it cools. Cool the custard completely and whisk in the crème fraîche. Refrigerate until very cold. Freeze in an ice cream maker according to the manufacturer's instructions.

Phyllo Cornets with Raspberries and Cream

Makes 6 cornets

Delicate and less rich than traditional cream horns, these festive pastries are delicious filled with raspberries and fresh cream. Dip the cornet points in melted milk chocolate and roll in crushed almonds for a more elaborate pastry.

6 sheets phyllo dough

5 tablespoons unsalted butter, melted

6 tablespoons raw or granulated sugar

2 cups heavy cream

½ cup confectioners' sugar

2 tablespoons raspberry eau-de-vie or
  other raspberry-flavored liqueur

1 cup fresh raspberries

Preheat the oven to 375 degrees F. Line a baking sheet with parchment paper or aluminum foil. Lightly spray 6 metal cream-horn molds with a vegetable-oil cooking spray.

Lay 1 sheet of phyllo dough flat on a clean work surface. Lightly butter the phyllo, working from the edges towards the center.

Cut the phyllo sheet lengthwise into four 3-by-17 ½-inch strips. Then cut each strip in half crosswise to create 8 strips in all. One at a time, wrap the buttered strips around a cream-horn mold until the entire surface of the mold is covered. Butter the cornet lightly and roll in 1 tablespoon of the raw or granulated sugar. Place the finished cornet on the prepared baking sheet. Repeat this process with the remaining phyllo sheets and cream-horn molds.

Bake the cornets until they are crisp and golden, 8 to 10 minutes. Remove them from the oven and allow them to

cool just until they can be handled. Carefully push each cornet off its mold. (Do this gently so that the phyllo isn't crushed.) Let the cornets cool completely before filling. The cornets can be stored for 1 or 2 days in a tightly covered container.

Chill a large mixing bowl and the beaters to an electric mixer for at least 15 minutes. Pour the cream into the chilled bowl. Press the confectioners' sugar through a sieve into the cream and stir in the eau-de-vie or other liqueur. Beat the cream at medium speed until soft peaks form. Increase the speed to high and continue beating until the cream forms firm peaks. Using a rubber spatula, spoon the cream into a pastry bag fitted with a large star tip.

Pipe a bit of the cream into the tip of each cornet. Reserving 6 perfect raspberries for garnish, divide the remaining berries among the 6 cornets. Pipe additional cream over the raspberries, filling the cornets and giving each one a 1-inch head of cream for garnish. Top each filled cornet with 1 raspberry and serve immediately.

Lemon Cream Mille-Feuilles

Fresh lemon curd lightened with whipped cream yields a butter-yellow mousse filling bursting with citrus flavor. Make sure the lemon curd is completely chilled before folding in the whipped cream.

For the pastry

6 sheets phyllo dough
5 tablespoons unsalted butter, melted
¾ cup confectioners' sugar
6 tablespoons ground pistachio nuts

For the lemon curd

3 large eggs
½ cup fresh lemon juice
2 tablespoons grated lemon zest
1 cup granulated sugar
6 tablespoons unsalted butter

1 cup heavy cream
Confectioners' sugar for sprinkling
Fresh raspberries or strawberries for garnish
6 sprigs fresh mint

To prepare the pastry, preheat the oven to 375 degrees F. Line a baking sheet with parchment paper.

Lay 1 sheet of phyllo dough flat on a clean work surface. Lightly butter the phyllo, working from the edges towards the center. Spoon the sugar into a small sieve and cover the buttered dough lightly with sugar. Sprinkle with 1 tablespoon of the pistachio nuts. Layer the remaining 5 sheets of phyllo, buttering and sprinkling each one.

Using a large, heavy baking sheet, press down on the layered phyllo gently but firmly to compress the sheets. Cut out 12 phyllo circles using a 3- to 3 ½-inch round cookie or biscuit cutter. Carefully transfer the circles to the baking sheet with a large metal spatula. Bake the phyllo for 5 to 7 minutes, or until the phyllo is crisp and golden. Transfer the pastries to wire racks to cool completely. (Phyllo circles can be stored in an airtight container for 1 or 2 days.)

To prepare the lemon curd, crack the eggs into a small bowl and beat well with a fork or small whisk. Combine the eggs with the lemon juice, zest, sugar, and butter in the top portion of a double boiler. (If a double boiler is unavailable, place the ingredients in a stainless steel bowl and place the bowl in a large sauté pan or skillet of simmering water.) Stir the lemon mixture constantly until the mixture thickens and coats the back of a spoon. Be careful not to let the mixture boil, or it will curdle.

Press the lemon curd through a sieve into a clean bowl. Cover the warm lemon curd with plastic wrap, pressing the wrap onto the surface to prevent a skin from forming on the curd. Chill until very cold, 3 to 4 hours.

Chill a large mixing bowl and the beaters of an electric mixer for about 15 minutes. Pour the cream into the chilled bowl and beat at medium-high speed until soft peaks form. Increase the speed to high and continue beating until the cream forms firm peaks. Using a large rubber spatula, carefully fold the whipped cream into the chilled lemon curd until smooth and well combined.

Spoon the lemon cream into a pastry bag fitted with a large star tip. Pipe approximately ½ cup of the cream onto 1 pastry circle. Place the pastry on a serving plate and top with a second pastry circle. Sprinkle with some confectioners' sugar and repeat the process for the remaining 5 servings. Garnish with raspberries or strawberries and a sprig of mint.

Pear and Praline Croustades

Amaretto and almond praline combine with tender pears to create a tempting combination in these individual dessert pastries. Serve the croustades with vanilla ice cream or sweetened vanilla whipped cream. They also make an extravagantly delicious breakfast served warm from the oven.

Praline
¾ cup granulated sugar
¾ cup slivered almonds

6 ripe, firm Bartlett or Comice pears, peeled,
   cored, and cut into ½-inch dice
2 or 3 tablespoons amaretto liqueur (to taste)

¼ teaspoon vanilla extract
2 tablespoons unsalted butter, cut into tiny
   chunks, plus 6 tablespoons (¾ stick)
   unsalted butter, melted
8 sheets phyllo dough
1 cup granulated sugar
Confectioners' sugar for sprinkling

To make the praline, lightly oil a baking sheet. In a small, heavy saucepan, melt the sugar over medium-high heat until it is a light golden color. Add the almonds and quickly stir to coat them with the sugar. Immediately pour the praline onto the baking sheet allowing it to cool completely and harden.

Break the praline into small chunks with your hands and put the chunks in a blender or food processor. Process until a coarse powder is formed.

In a large bowl, gently combine the pears with the praline powder, amaretto, vanilla extract, and butter chunks. Set aside.

Preheat the oven to 400 degrees F. Lightly spray a 12-cup muffin tin with vegetable-oil spray.

Lay 1 sheet of phyllo dough flat on a clean work surface. Brush the phyllo from the edges towards the center with some of the melted butter. Sprinkle with 2 tablespoons of the granulated sugar. Layer 3 more sheets of phyllo over the first, buttering and sprinkling each one. Using a sharp knife, cut the layers into six 5-inch squares, reserving any phyllo scraps. Repeat this process with the remaining 4 sheets of phyllo dough until there are twelve 5-inch squares and a pile of phyllo scraps.

Using a large spatula, carefully transfer a phyllo square to a muffin cup and gently press it in. The points of the dough should be sticking up. Repeat until all 12 muffin cups are lined with phyllo.

Spoon about ¼ cup of the pear filling into each phyllo-lined cup. Divide the phyllo scraps among the 12 pastries, carefully scrunching a few scraps over the pear filling to cover each one. Fold the edges of the phyllo squares over the filling, but do not press them flat. The tops of the pastries should have a crumpled dome shape. Sprinkle lightly with confectioners' sugar.

Bake for 25 to 30 minutes, or until the pastry is crisp, golden, and slightly caramelized. If the top of the phyllo begins to brown too quickly, cover lightly with a piece of aluminum foil and continue baking. Transfer the muffin pan to a wire rack to cool for 5 to 7 minutes. Using a small, narrow metal spatula, carefully transfer each crous-tade to a serving plate. (If the croustades appear golden brown but are still too soft and difficult to remove from the tins, let them cool for a few more minutes before removing.) Sprinkle the tops with confectioners' sugar.

Index

Table of Equivalents

Liquids

US	Metric	UK
2 tbl	30 ml	1 fl oz
¼ cup	60 ml	2 fl oz
⅓ cup	80 ml	3 fl oz
½ cup	125 ml	4 fl oz
⅔ cup	160 ml	5 fl oz
¾ cup	180 ml	6 fl oz
1 cup	250 ml	8 fl oz
1 ½ cups	375 ml	12 fl oz
2 cups	1 l	32 fl oz

Oven Temperatures

Fahrenheit	Celsius	Gas
250	120	½
275	140	1
300	150	2
325	160	3
350	180	4
375	190	5
400	200	6
425	220	7
450	230	8
475	240	9
500	260	10

Weights

US/UK	Metric
1 oz	30 g
2 oz	60 g
3 oz	90 g
4 oz (¼ lb)	25 g
5 oz (⅓ lb)	155 g
6 oz	185 g
7 oz	220 g
8 oz (½ lb)	250 g
10 oz	315 g
12 oz (¾ lb)	375 g
14 oz	440 g
16 oz (1 lb)	500 g
1 ½ lb	750 g
2 lb	1 kg
3 lb	1.5 kg

Length Measures

⅛ in	3 mm
¼ in	6 mm
½ in	12 mm
1 in	2.5 cm
2 in	5 cm
3 in	7.5 cm
4 in	10 cm
5 in	13 cm
6 in	15 cm
7 in	18 cm
8 in	20 cm
9 in	23 cm
10 in	25 cm
11 in	28 cm
12 in/1 ft	30 cm

The exact equivalents in the preceding tables have been rounded for convenience.